THE LITTLE BOOK OF FARTING

BY ALEC BROMCIE

Michael O'Mara Books Limited

First published in Great Britain in 1999 by
Michael O'Mara Books Limited
9 Lion Yard
Tremadoc Road
London SW4 7NQ

A CIP catalogue record for this book is available from
the British Library

ISBN 1-85479-445-0

5 7 9 10 8 6 4

Original concept and compilation by David Crombie
Edited by Helen Cumberbatch
Designed and typeset by DESIGN 23
Printed in England by William Clowes Ltd

ABOUT THE AUTHOR

Alec Bromcie is Visiting Professor of Wind and Sound at the University of Valparaiso. He is the author of many academic papers and theses on the subject of farting. His recent research into farting at high altitude won him the prestigious Yak Award from the University of Nepal. At present he is working on the development of a 'fartometer' – an appliance that can detect the source of a fart.

Contact Professor Bromcie by e-mail: alec.bromcie@michaelomarabooks.com

CONTENTS

*And suddenly there
came a sound from heaven
as of a rushing mighty wind,
and it filled all the house where
they were sitting.*

ACTS OF THE APOSTLES 2:2

THE TRUTH ABOUT FARTING

WHAT IS A FART?

Farts are nature's way of releasing our own toxins. Flatulence can be described as the pressure of excessive amounts of gas in the stomach or intestines. If we didn't release this pressure through farting, the gases we produce would be reabsorbed into the blood and poison us. And, as anyone who has ever suffered from trapped wind can verify, holding it in causes painful swelling and distension of the abdomen.

WHAT'S IN A FART?

Farts are mainly composed of five gases:

Nitrogen (N_2)
Hydrogen (H_2)
Carbon dioxide (CO_2)
Methane (CH_4)
Oxygen (O_2)

As hydrogen, nitrogen and oxygen are elements they will not give the true flavour of a fart by themselves. They need a bit of spicing up and must form compounds with carbon (C) and sulphur (S) e.g. hydrogen sulphide.

8

Did you know?

- NITROGEN predominates in farting by the formation of compounds such as indol and skatol. It is colourless, odourless, relatively unreactive and forms 78% of the air we breathe.

- HYDROGEN is the lightest and most abundant element in the universe. It is colourless, highly flammable and stinks when reacted with sulphur to form the compound hydrogen sulphide.

9

- CARBON DIOXIDE (or Carbon-acid gas) is a heavy, colourless gas which accounts for up to 50-60% of the gas in a fart. It is formed during respiration and the combustion of organic compounds. It dissolves in water to make carbonic acid, H_2CO_3, which is what makes drinks fizzy and, in turn, what results in bubbles in the bath! CO_2 is heavier than air so that its presence in a smelly fart causes the pong to linger longer...

- METHANE is also known as natural gas or marsh gas and is produced by the decomposition of organic matter. Since the food we eat also undergoes a process of decomposition (due to the action of *E. coli* microbes in the large bowel), and since food is almost entirely organic matter, it is not at all surprising that methane is present in farts. Methane is flammable and when lit will appear as a strong blue or green flame – DON'T TRY IT!!!!!

- OXYGEN is colourless, tasteless, odourless, highly reactive and essential for all aerobic respiration and almost all combustion. It is the commonest element in the Earth's crust and found in the compound CO_2 (see above). There are often only low levels of this gas in a fart but recycling is essential for human life.

- HYDROGEN SULPHIDE (rotten-egg gas) is colourless, inflammable, soluble in water and poisonous. This one's a real stinker . . .

HOW DO WE FART?

A fart begins with the swallowing of air, and as we all know what goes in must come out. The air travels down into the stomach where, initially, it is mainly composed of atmospheric nitrogen and oxygen. Some of the oxygen is absorbed, whilst the largely unabsorbable nitrogen continues through to the intestines. It is in the intestines that carbon dioxide, methane and hydrogen are formed. The carbon dioxide, produced by fermentation, is largely absorbed.

It is a fact of life that man (or woman) cannot fart on air alone. To make a decent fart, a loud, noisy, juicy or smelly one, he (she) needs some protein and some carbohydrate – i.e. some grub. During the digestion of food and the sorting out of the leftovers, bacteria ferment away, attacking the remains of our latest snack and blasting the food that has not been fully digested in the small or large intestine. At this point, the rest of the fart-inducing gases are produced.

Some foods prove harder to digest than others – i.e. foods which are rich in starch or cellulose such as cabbage – and these are the ones that farters love. The much-maligned baked bean, for example, is a complex carbohydrate that is just maldigested. And the same holds true for mushrooms, as mushrooms contain a sugar called raffinose, which humans can't break down. When the blend of gases (flatus) is ready for emission, the inevitable outcome is a FART!

NB: Gas, of course, is not the only result of Voidance (the act of ejection or evacuation). So for those that would prefer Avoidance of certain nasty accidents, do be careful where and when you let go. You have been warned....

HOW OFTEN DO WE FART?

Most of us pass somewhere between 200 and 2000ml of gas each and every day (an average voloume of about 600ml). An interesting thought for the next time that you breathe in a gulp of 'fresh' air.

On average we pass wind 10-20 times a day, and for men of about 20-40 years of age with healthily functioning bowels, the average number of gas eruptions is 16 times a day.

Did you know?

- It is possible to go a whole day without farting, but definitely not advisable
- The average man releases enough flatus in a day to blow up a small balloon
- The war of farting between the sexes is equal on all matters of sound and smell
- Average number of passages:
  Man: 15-17 farts in 24 hours
  Woman: 8-9 farts in 24 hours

Record farting statistics:

- 2000 ml
- 145 farts in 24 hours
- 70 farts in 4 hours

There is a cheat's method to farting and that is to suck back in the air after letting go a fart and then to release it again. In this way one draws air back into the colon and can fart and fart, and fart again.

WHY ARE SOME FARTS NOISY...

...and others quiet and deadly?

Vegetarians

Vegetarians fart more often than meat-eaters because their diet is harder to digest. They also fart more quietly as all that roughage loosens the sphincter muscles. Just for the record, the farts do tend to be particularly offensive to the nostrils. For those who'd prefer to have quiet farts, without turning veggie, let that air out very slowly and you might just get away with it.

Carnivores

Carnivores fart less than their veggie friends but, since they have tighter sphincters and go to the loo less often due to lack of roughage, they build up more pressure and hence are the greater reverberators. Squeezing the buttocks together may let out a fart bit by bit, but it can also result in a roaring blast. Be careful if you find yourself trying this in a lift or on a train at rush-hour.

WHY DO FARTS SMELL?

The disagreeable odour of flatus is caused by several sulphur compounds. Everyone has a different mixture of gases causing different smells (see chapter on WHAT'S IN A FART?) and some farts will contain greater amounts of heavy gas so that they will hang around longer than others.

Did you know?

- Like all good perfumes, after two minutes farts become odourless to our noses.

- If you fart into an airtight tin or into a bottle and put the cork back in, you can preserve your ripest farts for some time – although it is considered very anti-social to do this in someone else's flask or lunchbox.

HOW LONG IS A FART?

The length a fart hangs around depends on what foods one has eaten and how much gas has been expelled. Farts can travel as far as 50ft (15 metres) and the smell can linger for between two and five minutes, although farts of 20 minutes have been known.

CAN YOU EVER SEE A FART?

In a word, NO. (Unless you light one which doesn't really count.)

HOT FARTS

The heat of the moment can be very embarrassing – yes we all know the danger of hot farts! To understand why some farts are bum-burners we need to go back to our internal chemistry lab. Basically, if you have a very full intestine, the particles inside rush round more quickly than usual and in the process produce heat which hots up our gas. Some foods such as curry and chillies also affect the heat in our intestines – hence the power of the good old curry fart.

ARE BURPS THE SAME AS FARTS?

DEFINITELY NOT! Repeated belching indicates aerophagia (spasmodic swallowing of air). Some people with this problem can readily produce a series of belches on command. This form of belching is due to unconscious, repeated aspiration of air into the oesophagus, often in response to stress, followed by rapid expulsion.

FARTING ETIQUETTE

When and when not to drop one is a major problem that everyone at some time or other has to face up to. A common concern and a question I am often asked is 'I have just started going out with someone and I want to know when is the best time to introduce flatulence into the relationship?' Let's face it, we've all faced this problem at one time or another...!

Some people start as they mean to go on and let rip from day one of a new relationship. But most regard this behaviour as loutish and uncouth. Farting has to be carefully introduced into a relationship to allow both parties the freedom to express themselves. The list on the following pages includes some of the rules on etiquette to help readers through this social minefield.

THE RULES

1. After the fourth date you may feel relaxed enough to share with your partner what, up until now, has been held back for fear of rejection. Do not be tempted to let one rocket out which rattles the doors. The best way is to let a delicate flower of a fart escape from your cheeks, just loud enough for her to hear. Do not boast or show any pride in your fart; rather show horror and shame. At this point your partner will throw her arms around you and tell you not to worry.

The ice is broken and both of you can now fart together with ease.

Unfortunately, this rule does not apply to both sexes. As a woman, whatever you do, NEVER fart on a first date! Although this attitude may be regarded as sexist, it is essential that the man does it first. If you do thunder one out his poor masculinity will be brought into question and the relationship will be doomed. The only exception to this rule is if you are a policewoman or a prison warden. In that case it is entirely expected!

2. Fanny farts – how to respond. If the affair has already reached the point of freefall farting, then no problem! However, if not this may come as a great shock to some men. Ladies – fart warily and do try not to surprise him too soon. Men – should an involuntary rasp occur during lovemaking, be a man and neither recoil in horror nor laugh. Be sensitive to how your partner may be feeling and either ignore the parp or reassure your loved one. This way you can laugh long and loud about it with your mates for years to come.

3. Lifts and enclosed spaces are a definite no-no. You might like the odour of your farts but others will not.

4. Never fart near a fresh-food counter – not even an organic-food one. I was once in a supermarket by the fresh meat counter where some villain had just unloaded a motherload of putrid pong. A lady nearby was heard to exclaim, 'Do not buy their meat, it has obviously gone off.'

5. Never fart and then embrace your lover whilst wearing an overcoat on a cold day. As we know, hot air rises and your stench will travel upwards and emanate from underneath your coat lapels. Your embrace will be very short as the noxious substance hits your loved one's nostrils.

6. At work, never go into someone's office, drop one and then leave. This was done to me numerous times by a certain gentleman. The odour would linger so much that people coming in an hour later would exclaim, 'Martin's in today then!'

33

7. Farting in bed (blanket-ripping) and then pulling back the covers and sniffing one's own fart is a perfectly acceptable practice. However, pushing your loved one's head under (or Dutch-ovening) must rank as a crime against humanity! This is a very common male habit and I cannot stress enough that it is very unpleasant for the victim – I was as once subjected to it by a policewoman.

8. Never fart in the company of your mother-in-law/father-in-law.

9. If you are the sole occupant of a bath then farting is to be encouraged as it is a cheap way of enjoying a jacuzzi. However, farting in a bath whilst sharing it is not advisable. The effect of the hot water on the lower intestines is such that you could end up firing out a gust of gas and worse. There is nothing more embarrassing than sharing your bath with a partner and something rather unpleasant.

10. My last rule is the most important. You must take heed of this even if you ignore all my other rules. After six pints of beer and a chicken curry do NOT go to work wearing light coloured trousers. I am sure I do not need to spell it out for you. Your whole career could rest on keeping faithful to this vital rule.

THE DANGERS OF FARTING

I often get asked if farting is dangerous. The truth is farts are actually quite hygienic. They do not carry germs because the environment of the colon is acidic and any bacteria that do get through are harmless. So are farts dangerous? Here are my answers:

Yes: if farting on to a lit match. (DO NOT TRY THIS AT HOME)

Yes: if inhaled at close range. Inhaling farts will gradually poison one, causing light-headedness and headaches. So don't ride pillion on a motorcycle or hire a tandem if the person in front of you guzzled beans the night before.

Yes: if excessive. Gas in the intestine can cause considerable discomfort. It is commonly thought to cause abdominal pain, bloating, ballooning, distention, meteorism, voluminous abdomen, belching, or passage of excessively noxious farts.

Yes: during surgery. During digestive surgery or endoscopic surgery of the colon, the intestinal gas sometimes explodes in contact with the electric scalpel. In his book *The History of Farting*, Dr Benjamin Bart refers to a case in a Danish hospital in 1980. Surgeons were operating on a male patient when an electrical surgical knife ignited a pocket of intestinal gases. This set off an explosion which rippled its way through the poor fellow's digestive organs and, despite the best efforts of the surgeons, the patient died.

Yes: if trapped. Farts don't always find their passage to freedom and this can lead to a build-up of gas in the intestine resulting in trapped wind. Potentially this can be very painful, with the abdomen sometimes swelling so much that the sufferer feels they are about to explode!

40

Yes: if held in for too long. After a few hours all that gas will be trying to enter your blood system and poison you, so it's not a good idea to try it.

Yes: if farting in an enclosed space. After farting repeatedly in the same room for several hours you may well suffer a near-death experience. Reputedly, a man did once end his earthly days in such a pastime.

Curative measures:

- products as Deflatine, Wind-Eze and Beano (US) which are available from your local chemist
- chalk tablets – available over the counter or from your GP
- pineapple – the Indians used to eat pineapple after a meal to aid digestion
- peppermints – may help to settle the stomach – hence the after-dinner mint
- let go of your hang-ups and just let them rip!

Preventative measures:

- Don't overindulge on curry
- Don't exercise directly after a meal
- Don't become a vegetarian
- Don't go on a detox diet
- Chew your food
- Don't talk while eating
- Don't wear white underwear

FARTING PERSONALITIES

*'He was a real fart smeller –
uh, I mean a real smart feller'*

There are many types of people who fart every day. It's your job to identify them, point them out, and call them by name! (Assuming it wasn't you who did it, of course!) Here's a quick run-down of the type of people you're likely to catch farting around you on a daily basis:

THE AMBITIOUS FARTER:
One who's always in there first with a fart and quick to sniff out the competition.

THE DUTCH-OVEN FARTER:
One who farts in bed and then holds his partner's head under the bedclothes.

THE NOSY FARTER:
One who insists on sticking his nose into other people's farts.

45

THE OBSCENE FARTER:
One who pulls down his trousers before farting.

THE QUEASY FARTER:
One who farts and feels sick at the smell.

THE SNORKEL FARTER:
One who farts in the bath or swimming pool and then looks around for the fish.

THE UNFORTUNATE FARTER:
One who tries very hard to fart but shits himself instead.

THE XENOPHOBIC FARTER:
One who is afraid of farting in foreign places.

THE YIN/YANG FARTER:
One who tries to harmonise the positive and negative properties of a fart.

FARTING TYPES

It is often said that there are only two kinds of farts – your own, and someone else's, but in truth no two farts are the same. Farts differ from each other in terms of size, sound and smell. The list below describes a range of colourfully varied farts – how many do you recognise from both personal and passive experience?

BABLER BAZOOKA FART (or the Redhill Ripper): The sort of fart that will wake you up at night because it smells so bad! They can be silent or noisy, but they are the most fetid, repulsive, smelliest farts imaginable. In Transylvania, legend has it even the undead are repulsed by these. They're mostly dropped by women who try to keep them in, but it would be far better for all of us if they let rip frequently.

GREEN-LIGHT FART: A fart where the conditions make it perfect for it to be released. This one can be as long and loud as the issuer can make it. It rarely occurs in lifts, cars, boardrooms or public places.

HAY FEVER FART: Basically, you fart when you sneeze, but the catch is that you can't smell it.

50

IRREPRESSIBLE INTERNAL FART:
When you try to hold a fart in for too long, the Internal fart can be worse than the real thing (for you, not bystanders). It often sounds like heavy stomach growling. Not a true fart, but everyone knows that you will have to let it go soon. This fart will always make its way out eventually.

LORD-OF-THE-DANCE FART: In an attempt to cover up the sound of a fart, you switch the topic of conversation to *Lord of the Dance* and start to stamp your feet loudly on the ground. Whilst you are doing this, you let one escape without anyone noticing.

MORNING FART: The 'first-thing-out-of-bed' fart. Long, loud and not too smelly; very satisfying to release all that gas after the night-time build-up.

ORGANIC FART: The person who farts an Organic fart is usually heavily into health foods and may even ask if you noticed how good, pure and healthy his fart smells. It may smell to you like any other fart, but there is no harm in agreeing with him. He is doing what he thinks is best.

QUESTIONING FART: This fart starts out low, and rises in pitch towards its conclusion, sounding as if your arse is asking a question.

SADDAM HUSSEIN FART: (also known as 'the mother of all farts') Chemical warfare has begun. You must call CNN and send for United Nation inspectors owing to the huge scale of the potential outbreak.

UNDERWATER FART: Often done in the bath, or while swimming. It bears an uncanny resemblance to the sound made by the engine of a nuclear submarine. Can be smelt on rising to the surface, and experienced windbreakers will often catch the fart in an upturned jam-jar, in order to set light to it.

VIAGRA FART: After a long slow fart, you feel yourself aroused.

YOGIC FART: An inevitable by-product of athletic yogic positions and intense concentration. As both the mind and body are focused on supreme relaxation and control, one's ability to monitor the passage of internal gases becomes impaired, and the inevitable occurs.

WISE WORDS ON WIND

I always have a quotation at my fingertips for every occasion (if it's to do with farting). Here are just a few of them – some of the wisest words ever spoken on the subject . . .

Quando il malato scoppia, il medico plange! (When the sick man farts, the doctor cries!)
Old saying from southern Italy, akin to the English saying 'An apple a day keeps the doctor away.'

It is best for flatulence to pass without noise and breaking, though it is better for it to pass with noise than to be intercepted and accumulated internally.

HIPPOCRATES, C. 460–C. 357 BC

All citizens shall be allowed to pass gas whenever necessary.

CLAUDIUS CAESAR

May the wind be always at your back.

ANONYMOUS

This too shall pass...

ABRAHAM LINCOLN

58

A man may break a word with you, sir; and words are but wind; Ay; and break it in your face, so he break it not behind.

WILLIAM SHAKESPEARE,
THE COMEDY OF ERRORS

What comfort can the vortices of Descartes give to a man who has whirlwinds in his bowels?

BENJAMIN FRANKLIN

It's an ill wind that blows nobody any good.

PROVERB

What winde can there blowe,
that doth not some man please?
A fart in the blowyng
doth the blower ease.

JOHN HEYWOOD

Oaths are but words,
and words but wind.

SAMUEL BUTLER, *HUDIBRAS*

Blow, winds, and crack your cheeks!
rage! blow!

WILLIAM SHAKESPEARE, *KING LEAR*

For the gentle wind does move
Silently, invisibly.

WILLIAM BLAKE

The wind bloweth where it listeth,
and thou hearest the sound thereof,
but canst not tell whence it cometh,
and whither it goeth.

BIBLE, ST JOHN 3:8

Not I, not I, but the wind that blows
through me!

D.H. LAWRENCE,
SONG OF A MAN WHO HAS COME THROUGH

The wind in a man's face makes him wise

S. PALMER
MORAL ESSAYS ON PROVERBS

When the wind's in the north,
You mustn't go forth.

DENHAM, *PROVERBS*

The winds of the daytime wrestle and fight
Longer and stronger than those of the night.

ANON

I should like one of these days to be so well known, so popular, so celebrated, so famous, that it would permit me . . . to break wind in society, and society would think it a most natural thing.

HONORÉ DE BALZAC, FRENCH NOVELIST

Chevy Chase couldn't ad-lib a fart after a baked-bean dinner.

JOHNNY CARSON, US CHAT-SHOW HOST

Gerry Ford is so dumb that he can't fart and chew gum at the same time.

LYNDON B. JOHNSON, US PRESIDENT

Acting is largely a matter of farting about in disguises.

PETER O'TOOLE, BRITISH ACTOR

I have more talent in my smallest fart than you have in your entire body.

WALTER MATTHAU TO BARBRA STREISAND

FARTING EUPHEMISMS

A sigh is but a breath of air that
issues from the heart;
But when it takes a DOWNWARD
course, it's simply called a FART!

The act of 'farting' and the resulting
'fart' can be expressed in many
different ways. The following pages
contain a colourful range of farting
euphemisms and synonyms – essential
knowledge for the committed farter.

TO FART (vb)

Backfire
Bark
Bip
Blast
Blow off
Blow the ol' butt
  trumpet
Break wind
Breeze
Cough
Crack a rat
Cut the cheese
Draw mud
Drop a shoe
Drop one's guts
Fire a Scud missile
Flatulate
Float an air biscuit
Fluff
Frame
Grep
Guff
Honk
Janet
Let off
Let one rip

Ming	Rosebud
Pass wind	Rumble
Pier	Shoot a bunny
Poop	Step on a duck
Pot	Totter
Proof	Trump
Queef	Woof

FART (n.)

Afterburner	Exploding turd
Anal audio	Explosion
Barking spider	Firecracker
Bench warmer	Flatulence
Blow-hole	Gravy pants
Bottom burp	Happy honker
Botty burp	Mud duck
Butt burner	Natural gas
Butt blast	Nature's little surprise
Butt sneeze	Nature's musical box
Cheek flapper	Raspberry tart
Cheeser	Rat bark
Crack splitter	Ripper

S.A.V. – Silent and Violent
S.B.D. – Silent but Deadly
Shit siren
Shit snore
Sidewinder
Stinker
Thunder from down under
Trouser cough
Trouser ripper
Under thunder
Wet one

FARTING ALL OVER THE WORLD

Essential Farting Phrases for Travellers

When travelling around the world to farting conferences, I often find certain farting phrases indispensable. Here are some handy phrases for beer-drinking curry eaters who find themselves adrift on foreign turf!

When in France:

Auriez-vous un masque?
Have you got a mask?

Ça sent pas la rose!
It smells. Or, literally, it doesn't smell like a rose.

Où sont les toilettes? Je ne me sens pas bien.

Where is the toilet? I don't feel well.

Où se trouvent les toilettes pour femmes?

Where's the ladies?

Je n'arrive pas à ouvrir les fenêtres.

I can't get these windows open.

When in Sweden:

Er hund har visst fisit igen.
Your dog seems to have farted again.
(meaning 'Yes, it was me, but I'd
rather blame it on an innocent
animal.')

*Var vänlig visa mig till avdelningen
för pruttkuddar.*
Please point me to the whoopee-
cushion department.

Hur mycket lök får jag för en tia?
How many onions will £1 get me?

Är det mycket vitlök i den här grytan?
Does this stew contain a lot of garlic?

Man ska vädra sina åsikter.
One should give air to one's opinions.

When in Spain:

¡Quiero tirarme un pedo!
I want to fart!

¿Donde se puede comer un buen curry?
Where can I get a good curry?

¡Huele muy mal!
That smells terrible!

¿Donde estan los servicios?
Where is the loo?

¡Ten cuidado, mi perro va a eliminar gases!
Be careful, my dog is about to break wind!

When in South Africa:

Waar kan ek 'n kerrie ëet?
Where can I get a good curry?

Dit luik heerlik!
That's a wonderful smell!

Ek wil boentjies vir aandete he.
I want beans for supper.

Ek het te veel blomkool geëet.
I've eaten too much cabbage.

Dit luik sleg!
That smells terrible!

When in Italy:

Questa birra tedesca mi fa scureggiare come una tromba!
This German beer is making me fart like a trumpet!

Lui ha appena fatto una puzza della Madonna!
He's just done a really smelly one!

Le tre scuregge: (The Three Farts)

1. *Siquam: silenziosa quasi mortale*
– silent but deadly/violent

2. *Tadem: tanfo della madonna*
– a really smelly one

3. *Bosef: boato senza fetore*
– a thunderer

When in Poland:

To smierdzi okropnie w tym pokoju.
It smells bad in this room.

Ten gulasz jest ostry!
This goulash is spicy!

Ta zupa z kapusty jest dobra.
This cabbage soup is good.

Chciaiabym jajko na smiadarnie.
I would like four eggs for breakfast.

NO LAUGHING MATTER

I couldn't resist lowering the tone of this book by sharing with readers some of my favourite farting jokes of all time – and, just like a fart, the best ones hang around the longest. Honk as loud as you like!

FART – a belch that didn't find the lift.
BELCH – a fart that caught the lift.

How can you tell if a woman is
wearing tights?
If she farts her ankles blow up.

Why do farts smell?
So deaf people can enjoy them too.

What is the definition of a fart?
A turd honking for the right of way.

What do you get when you've been eating onions and beans?
Tear gas.

Q: What's the definition of a surprise?
A: A fart with a lump in it.

Two old maids were discussing the merits of tights. 'I don't like them at all,' said one. 'Every time I fart it blows my slippers off.'

It was so cold in the mountains that Old Jake woke one morning to find two ice cubes in his sleeping bag. When he threw them on the fire they went: Phartsst! Pharsst!

Tarzan, who lived entirely on jungle vegetables, was greeted by his lady friend with the wrinkled-nose exclamation: 'You! Tarzan – Methane!'

Stepping into the elevator the businessman quickly detected an offensive odour. The only other occupant was a little old lady. 'Excuse me,' he addressed her, 'did you happen to pass wind?' 'Of course I did,' she replied. 'You don't think I stink like this all the time do you?'

At the annual barndance Mr Brown set a new record when he ate 40 plates of baked beans. However the record was not counted due to a following wind.

A guy walks into a bar and bets the barman £20 that he can fart the national anthem. When the bartender agrees, the guy jumps up on the bar, squats, drops his pants and shits all over the bar... The barman goes nuts and yells 'What the hell are you doing?' The farter explains, 'Hey, even Pavarotti has to clear his throat before a performance!!!'

The Queen was showing the
Archbishop of Canterbury around her
new stables when a stallion nearby let
go such a resounding fart it rattled the
windows and couldn't be ignored.
'Oh dear,' said the Queen, blushing,
'I'm frightfully sorry about that.'
'Think nothing of it, Ma'am,' said the
archbishop. 'All actions are God-given.
But anyway, I thought it was the
stallion.'

A Scotsman was so mean the only way he would take a bubble bath on Saturday morning was to eat baked beans for his supper on Friday night.

A man stops his car in the high street, gets out and takes a leak in the gutter. A policeman spots him and fines him £15 on the spot. The man gives him a £20 note but the policeman finds that he hasn't any change. 'Oh keep it,' says the man, getting back in his car. 'After all, I've just farted as well.'

Three men had a competition to see who could run the longest without farting. The first farted after 25 metres, the second after 50 metres and the third collapsed after a mile without having farted at all. 'How did you manage it?' asked the other two. 'Easy, I stuck a cork up my bum.'

A man at the bar farts very loudly. Another man then taps him on the shoulder and says, 'Excuse me but you just farted in front of my wife!' 'I apologise,' says the culprit. 'I didn't realise it was her turn.'

In the geriatrics ward, old Ben was dozing in his chair. Every time he leaned to one side a nurse would gently push him straight. A new patient arrived and asked how he found being in the ward: 'Oh it's all right,' said old Ben. 'But that young nurse makes it bloody difficult for one to have a fart.'

An air-freshener seller gets into a lift where she is overcome by a rumbly tummy and lets go a shocker of a fart. 'Ah ha' she thinks, 'no worries,' and takes out one of her samples of pine freshener and gives it a liberal spray. At the next floor a man gets in. 'Christ,' he says, 'What's that smell?' The lady replies: 'Oh, that's my pine air-freshener.' 'Pine air-freshener?' chokes the man. 'It smells more like someone shat on a Christmas tree.'

There is a young yachtsman from Wales,
Whose boating technique never fails.
He dines on baked beans
And plenty of greens,
So his farts put the wind in his sails.

There was an old lady from Crewe
Who was constantly stricken with flu.
She'd cough herself hoarse
And sneeze with such force,
That she'd often let off a few too!

There was an old geezer from Devon
Who'd fart on the stroke of eleven.
With baked beans for brunch
And poached eggs for lunch,
He'd be parping till quarter-past seven.

There once was a fellow from Louth
Whose farts would escape from his mouth.
He tried every night
To reverse their flight
But regardless, they never flew South.

If you enjoyed this little book, you'll love
the other 'Little Book' titles published by
Michael O'Mara Books Ltd:

The Little Book of Pants
ISBN 1-85479-477-9

The Little Book of Stupid Men
ISBN 1-85479-454-X

The Little Toilet Book
ISBN 1-85479-456-6

The Little Book of Venom
ISBN 1-85479-446-9

If you would like more information,
please contact our UK Sales Department:

Fax: 020 7 622 6956

E-mail: jokes@michaelomarabooks.com